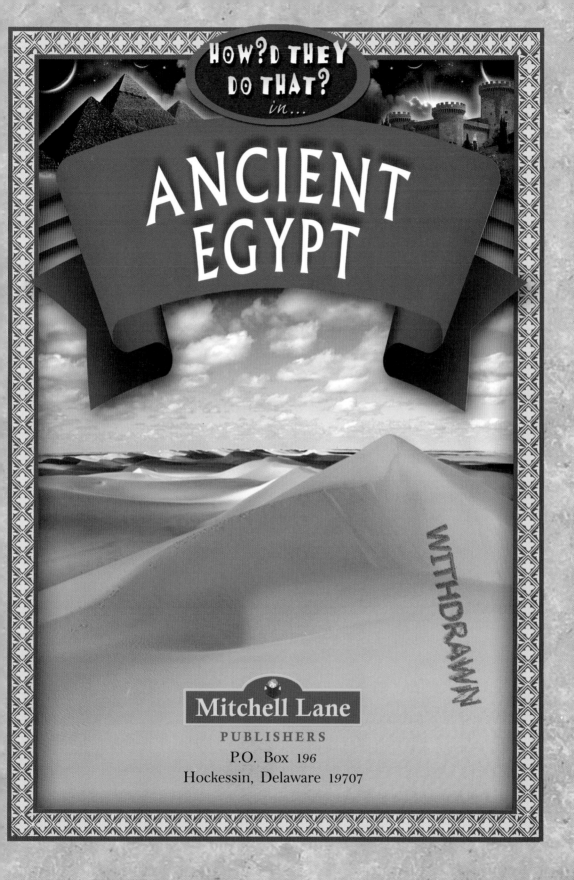

HOW?D THEY DO THAT? *in...*

ANCIENT EGYPT

Mitchell Lane
PUBLISHERS

P.O. Box 196
Hockessin, Delaware 19707

HOW?'D THEY DO THAT? *in...*

Ancient Egypt

Ancient Greece

Ancient Mesopotamia

Ancient Rome

The Aztec Empire

Colonial America

Elizabethan England

The Mayan Civilization

The Persian Empire

Pre-Columbian America

HOW?D THEY
DO THAT?

in...

ANCIENT
EGYPT

TAMRA ORR

Mitchell Lane

PUBLISHERS

Printing   2   3   4   5   6   7   8   9

Library of Congress Cataloging-in-Publication Data
Orr, Tamra.
  How'd they do that in ancient Egypt / by Tamra Orr.
      p. cm.—(How'd they do that)
  Includes bibliographical references and index.
  ISBN 978-1-58415-821-9 (library bound)
  1. Egypt—Civilization—To 332 B.C.—Juvenile literature. I. Title.
  DT61.O66 2010
  932–dc22

                                                        2009027339

AUTHOR'S NOTE: The symbol 𓂀 is the Eye of Horus.

PUBLISHER'S NOTE: This story is based on the author's extensive research, which she believes to be accurate. Documentation of his research is on page 60.

To reflect current usage, we have chosen to use the secular era designations BCE ("before the common era") and CE ("of the common era") instead of the traditional designations BC ("before Christ") and AD (*anno Domini*, "in the year of the Lord").

The internet sites referenced herein were active as of the publication date. Due to the fleeting nature of some web sites, we cannot guarantee they will all be active when you are reading this book.

                                                        PPC/PLB4

CONTENTS

Under the Egyptian Sun 6
FYInfo: The Divine Nile 11
1   Time for Work and Play 13
    FYInfo: The Game of Senet 17
2   Growing Up Egyptian 19
    FYInfo: The Rosetta Stone 23
3   At Home 25
    FYInfo: Up on the Roof 29
4   For the Gods 31
    FYInfo: The Job of Tears 35
5   Life with the Pharaoh 37
    FYInfo: Egyptian Slaves 43
6   Looking Good 45
    FYInfo: Egyptian Makeup 49
7   Beyond Death 51
    FYInfo: Making Mummies 55

Craft: Make an Egyptian Reed Boat 56
Timeline 58
Further Reading 60
    Books 60
    Works Consulted 60
    On the Internet 60
Glossary 61
Index 62

The first ray of sun peeked over the horizon. Daylight had returned once more to ancient Egypt.

As the sky slowly lit up with the soft colors of dawn, everyone in Nomti's family was already stirring. It was *Shemu*, the harvest season, and no one was allowed to linger for a moment in a warm bed. It was time to do nothing other than work, work, work. No one slid into a car or climbed aboard a bus. Work was close by, so all they had to do was walk.

Yawning, Nomti walked out of her house and joined the others on their way to labor in the grain fields. "Good morning, Nomti," her mother said, with a smile. Her parents would work with her today, as always. Her brother, Wati, and sister, Shamise, would, too. Slaves would toil alongside army soldiers, craftsmen next to bakers. At this time of year, the nobles were the only people not found in the fields.

Nomti did not need to be reminded why everyone had to work so hard. It was not for a weekly paycheck or a bonus. Money did not exist

in ancient Egypt. Instead, Nomti's family, and everyone she knew, worked because they would be paid for their efforts in grain and other produce—enough supplies to keep their families from going hungry for the rest of the year. Nomti also knew that she had to move fast, before the summer heat began. The high temperatures would make the tiring work even more challenging, plus she needed enough time to harvest the grain and then repair the irrigation ditches before the divine Nile River rose again and brought the floodwaters back.

Farmers have it much easier today than those in ancient Egypt. Harvesting grain now is a simpler process because farmers use huge machines called harvester-threshers. This modern equipment can easily cut more than 40 acres a day—something it took many Egyptians days to do.

As the sun kept rising in the sky, bringing its powerful light and heat, Nomti wiped the sweat off her face and wondered how long before she could take the first break of the morning and have a chance to

A mural in a burial chamber shows a man plowing his fields. These same farming techniques have been used for centuries, although the animals pulling the plows have changed over time.

eat something. She watched as an overseer walked down the row, making sure that everyone under his command was keeping up. He got angry whenever he saw anyone stopping to rest.

Nomti's father was in front of her. Using a sharp instrument called a sickle, he cut ears of corn and dropped them on the ground. Nomti, Wati, Shamise, and their mother followed him, gathering the ears into bundles called sheaves. Some of the cornstalks were left standing in the fields. Nomti knew that they would be used later to feed the livestock.

It was backbreaking work, and Nomti could already feel her muscles beginning to complain. Behind her mother walked the poorer families. They were searching for any grain that Nomti's family might have missed and they could take home.

At the end of the field, Nomti could see two of her friends. They carried a long stick that stretched between their shoulders. A heavy sack hung down in the middle. It was full of corn and would be carried to the threshing floor, where the corn would be cleaned and measured.

Nomti wished she could join them, but she still had endless ears to bend over and pick up. After standing up to stretch, she got back to work. It would be a long day . . . week . . . month until the harvesting was done. But Nomti smiled as she thought of the food it would bring to her family. All of the work was well worth having enough to eat.

Harvesttime, usually between March and June, was a period of intense work from sunrise to sunset for the ancient Egyptians. All crops, from corn and grain to cucumbers and watermelons, had to be brought in before the waters of the Nile began to rise and flood the area again. It took almost everyone working together to make sure it got done.

When the floodwaters came, everyone rested and enjoyed a time of celebration. Then, as soon as the waters went back between the

Many of the traditions used by ancient Egyptians are still used in fields today. A young boy and girl may spend hours out in the fields, harvesting crops.

riverbanks, leaving behind rich, fertile mud, the work began again. First, seeds were planted in the moist ground. The Egyptians placed the seeds on the ground and then drove sheep over them, which buried the seeds. The main tools farmers used were hoes and sickles. They also used plows made out of bow-shaped sticks that they dragged across the ground or attached to strong workers, who would pull them.

Farming was one of the most important jobs in ancient Egypt. The Egyptians grew wheat, barley, flax, lettuce, melons, onions, celery, squash, garlic, figs, dates, and grapes. They also grew many different herbs for spicing their foods, such as mint, dill, rosemary, sage, and thyme. Extra produce was used to trade with other communities up and down the Nile. Wheat might be exchanged for timber or horses from the east, or for salt, copper, or gold from the desert.

Although much of Egypt was dry, sandy, and desolate, the areas on either side of the Nile River were perfect for growing crops. The desert area was known as the "red land," while the people lived in the "black land." The rhythm of the Nile guided every aspect of life in ancient Egypt.

The waters of the Nile were put to good use. When the summer heat dried the ground, there were no sprinklers to set up or hoses to untangle. Instead, the Egyptians dug long canals or ditches leading into the fields from the river. By using a system of gates and dikes, they could hold this water back until they

A shadoof

needed it. They also created a tool called a shadoof. It was a long pole with a weight attached to one end and a leather bag or reed basket on the other. The bag or basket was dipped into the water, and then, using a little strength and the counterweight, tipped up and into the ditch or onto the field.

Life in ancient Egypt was demanding—but as full of hard work as it was, it also had moments of fun and celebration. In that way, the past and the present are very much alike!

The Divine Nile

The Nile River is the longest river in the world, reaching over 4,000 miles from East Africa to the Mediterranean. It snakes through nine modern countries. For the ancient Egyptians, the Nile was far more than just a huge river. It was life itself, and it was considered divine.

Life in Egypt would not have been possible without the Nile. The river brought the mud that turned into fertile soil for planting crops. It provided the water that helped plants grow. Since Egypt was terribly hot and surrounded by sand, the Nile's water was the source for drinking, cooking, and bathing. It helped with sanitation. It also brought food as people caught turtles, clams, fish—and even crocodiles—for dinner.

When the Nile flooded each year, it made it possible for life to go on for the Egyptian people. If it did not flood enough, crops would die, and people would starve. If it flooded too much, it washed away homes, crops, and even families.

The Nile helped the Egyptians measure the passing of time. Its depth and flow told them whether a time of plenty or a time of suffering was coming. The Egyptians even invented a device called the nilometer, which measured water levels. The instrument was a wall of stone with marks on it, much like a giant ruler. Flights of steps bordered it, and Egyptians could regularly climb down the steps to check whether the water level was rising or falling.

Since most travel was done by boat, the Nile was also like an Egyptian superhighway. Boats of all shapes and sizes traveled it constantly. Small rafts made of reeds carried goods from one part of the community to another. Larger boats ferried people from place to place. Huge freighters loaded with grain or cattle were sent downriver for trade. Fancy boats carried nobles onto the water to catch the cool evening breeze. Gigantic 200-foot barges even carried stone pillars for constructing huge buildings like temples and pyramids. The Nile brought food and other goods to the people, reminding them that without the divine river, they would not be able to survive.

The Nile River

The Seated Scribe *sculpture, from the fourth or fifth dynasty of Egypt, 2600–2350 BCE, is painted limestone. Its eyes are rock crystal in copper.*

TIME FOR WORK AND PLAY

Chapter 1

As important as farming was to the Egyptians, it was not the only job to be done. What kind of job you had greatly depended on what class you and your family fit into.

The nobles, people related in some way to the pharaoh and his family, did not work much at all. The viziers, or priests, focused on giving the pharaoh advice and guidance as well as taking special daily care of the statues in the temples. Below them came people who had specialized training, such as doctors, magicians, and tax collectors. Underneath them came the scribes, then soldiers, craftsmen, farmers, and finally the slaves and servants.

Keeping Records

One of the most important jobs in ancient Egypt was that of a scribe. Only four out of 1,000 Egyptians were able to read or write, so being able to do so was both an honored skill and a holy process. It was considered a gift from Thoth, the god of wisdom.

The smartest young boys were sent to a special school within the temples to learn how to write. They did not practice writing 26 letters of the alphabet on pieces of paper like modern students do in school.

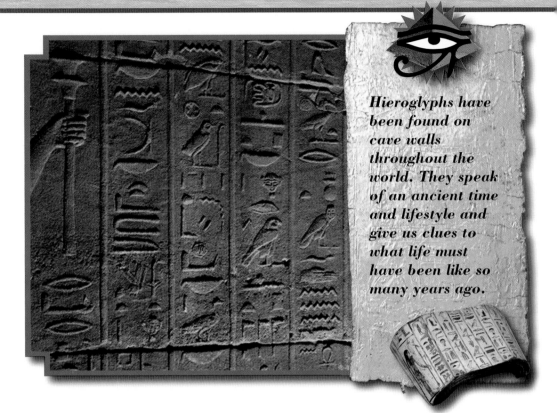

Hieroglyphs have been found on cave walls throughout the world. They speak of an ancient time and lifestyle and give us clues to what life must have been like so many years ago.

Instead, they learned more than 700 hieroglyphs—symbols that represented letters and sounds. They practiced them every single day with red and black ink and brushes made from reeds. Papyrus was too precious to use for practicing, so students worked with slabs of rock instead.

It took years to learn how to be a good scribe. Once you knew the skills, though, you were guaranteed a great job working as a secretary for the pharaoh or the nobles, as a priest, or as a doctor. What did the scribes write? Anything they were told to! They recorded important events like great battles and simple daily prayers. They wrote down the most popular stories, songs, and poems. They kept track of business dealings and wrote letters for those who did not know how.

Crafts

Do you like to dress up and find ways to look special? The Egyptians sure did. They loved to wear makeup, wigs, and jewelry. Many craftsmen kept busy making these luxuries. Gold and gems were plentiful in

Egypt, so it was common for noble men and women to wear necklaces, bracelets, and anklets embedded with precious stones like turquoise and amethyst. Ivory was used for decorating furniture and cosmetic boxes. Alabaster was used for small vases that held scented oil and perfumes. Weavers, stoneworkers, and potters kept busy as well. While weavers made fine linen for clothes, potters created dishes, jars, and mugs from clay, and stoneworkers made plates, bowls, and vases.

Of course, the pharaoh and his family wore many beautiful jewels and gold. A number of ancient drawings show them with beaded head-dresses and shiny golden necklaces. Almost everyone wore amulets—necklaces that were thought to protect the wearer from evil spirits. The commoners wore amulets made of wood, stone, and bone, while those of nobles were made of gold and embedded with jewels.

Egyptian carpenters made everything from small toys to coffins. Cobblers made sandals to protect people's feet. Butchers slaughtered animals and preserved the meat. Fishermen caught and dried fish. Poulterers caught birds in nets and traps and sold them for dinner.

There were other jobs available for Egyptians. Some of the most exhausting and dangerous ones involved working in the mines and quarries. In the fields, herders watched over cattle, goats, and sheep. Marshmen spent their days in the water, fishing, hunting, and gathering papyrus, which would later be turned into a type of writing paper.

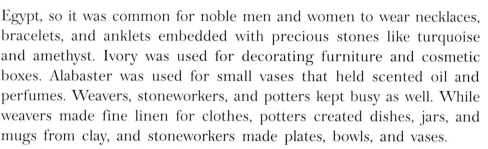

Let's Play

Even though the people spent a great deal of time working, there was time for play, too. Some of the toys Egyptian

Egyptian toy

Taking time to play was as popular then as it is today!

children played with are like those used today. Kids tossed clay and wooden balls or practiced juggling them; made up stories about their dolls and toy animals; and even played with spinning tops.

Egyptian kids also played some of the same physical games that kids do now. They would grab a rope and start a round of tug of war, give each other piggyback rides, and challenge one another in arm wrestling. Without television or books to keep them entertained, they told each other stories, like "The Shipwrecked Sailor" or "The Doomed Prince."

One of their favorite games was similar to monkey-in-the-middle. First, everyone sat down in a circle. One child sat in the center. Next, the kids on the outside stuck their feet into the circle and tried to touch the person on the inside. If the one in the middle could grab someone else's toes, then that person became "it" and had to take a turn in the middle.

Another favorite was a game like hockey. It used long palm branches for sticks and a puck made of two pieces of leather with papyrus stuffed in between them.

Nebamun, a noble, hunts fowl in the marshes.

Grown-ups enjoyed the chance to relax too. They would play board games, or they'd go out on the Nile for a boatride to enjoy cool breezes. Others found a much more active way to have fun—they went hunting. Armed with wooden spears and arrows, they would go into the desert with their hunting dogs and guides to hunt for gazelle, antelope, foxes, and lions. Still others spent their free time making music. They played harps, drums, flutes, lyres, and mandolins.

The Game of Senet

Senet board inscribed with the name of Amenhotep III

One of the most popular board games in ancient Egypt was senet. Rich and poor, young and old enjoyed this game, which is similar to backgammon. Over the years, as many as 50 senet sets have been found buried in tombs, some of them in near perfect condition. The fact that they were included in burial chambers is a sign of how important this game was to some people.

No one is sure when or how senet was invented. It is old, though! A wall painting dating back to 2650 BCE shows people playing the game together.

Even though a number of senet games have been discovered, the rules of the game remain a mystery. The board itself was made up of 30 squares in three rows of ten. Certain squares had special markings on them. The markings told the player what he could and could not do. For example, landing on the square with a bird on it could have meant you had to stop; three wavy lines that you had to go backward; and three circles that you had to roll a three before you could move on.

The game pieces that move around the board are called pawns. They came in different shapes such as pyramids, cones, or barrels. Each player had between five and ten pawns. Where and how much they moved was determined either by throwing four flat-sided sticks or by dice made out of bone.

Several people have tried to figure out what the rules of the game might have been. Winning seemed to center on being the first player to reach the Kingdom of Osiris and get their pieces off the board. No matter how the game was played, one thing was sure: Everyone wanted to play!

This bronze statue is one of the many cat images found in Egyptian tombs. Cats were considered sacred and spiritual animals by Egyptian royalty, and their mummies were often included in their royal tombs.

GROWING UP EGYPTIAN

Chapter 2

Do you spend much time with your family? Between school, chores, friends, homework, and sleep, it can be difficult to see your parents or siblings for more than an hour or two a day. In ancient Egypt, it was quite different. Families spent a great deal of time together. Since so many of the infants died before they turned one year old, babies were precious. Egyptian mothers did not have day care centers or babysitters. Instead they would carry their babies around with them in slings until the children were old enough to walk.

Most children did not go to school. Their families could not afford to send them. Parents did not have to leave the house to work eight hours a day. Many homes included parents and children, as well as aunts, uncles, and grandparents. A pet dog, cat, or monkey was not unusual, either.

Boys and girls sometimes played together, but for the most part, they went their separate ways. Boys began going to work with their fathers by the age of four and learned their trade or craft. Four-year-old girls, on the other hand, began learning how to run a household. Their mothers showed them how to sew, cook, and clean.

"The lock of youth"

One thing that neither boys nor girls had to worry much about when growing up was what to wear. Until they became teenagers, they did not wear anything at all. Since it was so hot in Egypt, it was the easiest way to stay cool. Boys often shaved their heads except for one spot where they had a pony-tail that they wore over their right ear. It was called "the lock of youth." It kept boys cooler in the heat. Girls had long hair but kept it in a braid so that it was out of their way. They often added beads, stones, or ribbons to make their hair look pretty.

Families ate their meals together, and when it was time for fun, they often did that together, too. They might go fishing out in the marshes with spears and nets. On a hot day, they might climb into a small reed boat and go sailing for some cool air.

Time to Celebrate!

Several times a year, families would gather for important festivals. These celebrations were held to honor births, deaths, harvests, new pharaohs, and other happy events. For example, during the time of year when the Nile River flooded and there was not much work to do, people would go to the Beautiful Feast of Opet. It lasted an entire month! At the Karnak Temple, people would gather to watch as a jeweled, golden statue of the god Amun was placed upon a sacred boat and sent down the river. As it passed by, people could shout out important questions that they wanted answered. If the answer was yes, the ship would tip forward. If it was no, the ship tipped backward. The Egyptians also took the opportunity to beg the god for favors and make wishes.

During the summer, just in time for harvest, families went to the Beautiful Feast of the Valley. It honored the Egyptians' dead relatives

At Karnak Temple, a statue of Amun soars up to the sky to watch over his people. He was often considered to be the king of the gods.

and ancestors. They wanted to make sure that those who had passed were doing well in the afterlife. Entire families visited the tombs of the dead and brought flowers, food, and drink as offerings. They stayed around to help eat the food and then spent the night there in order to be close to the souls of their loved ones. Family was important to all Egyptians—whether the members were alive or not.

Time to Grow Up

Adulthood came early in Egypt. By the time girls were thirteen years old and boys were eighteen, they were getting married. That probably seems very young, but keep in mind that people lived only to the age of forty or so back then. They had to start young in order to have time to work and have children.

Although religion and honoring the gods were very important to Egyptians, getting married was not a religious ceremony. Instead it was a legal one. Husbands and wives had equal rights and shared ownership of their home and belongings. Children were eagerly awaited—and the circle of life continued.

A wedding ceremony on the Nile

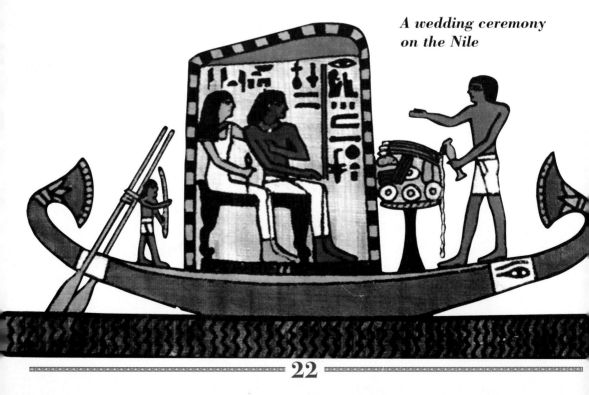

The Rosetta Stone

Imagine the excitement of finding hundreds of messages from people who lived long, long ago. What could those messages teach you about what life was like then? Now imagine the frustration of not being able to read or understand those messages. That is what happened when explorers found hieroglyphs. They could tell that the symbols meant something, but they had no idea what.

All that changed in 1799. French troops, sent by Napoleon Bonaparte, were digging the foundation for a fort in Lower Egypt. They found a black slab of stone. It had very strange markings all over it. It seemed important—and it was.

Thanks to the hard work of British physicist Thomas Young and French Egyptologist Jean François Champollion, the markings on the stone were translated. Over time, experts discovered that there were three different languages written on the stone. One was formal Greek. One was demotic, an everyday style of Greek. Scholars understood this language, and

The Rosetta Stone

they knew how to translate it. The third language was Egyptian hieroglyphs. The experts figured out that the stone had the same information on it in all three languages. By knowing what one meant, they could figure out the others. Suddenly, all of those picture symbols engraved on stones and painted on cave walls began to make sense.

The Rosetta Stone is kept at the British Museum. It has been there since 1802. The stone and all that it represents have become so well known that even the phrase *rosetta stone* has come to mean anything that is used to unlock a mystery. Some businesses use the name to sell programs that teach people how to speak other languages.

Ancient Egyptians lived in mud-brick homes in the desert town of Siwa Oasis. The town has gone by many names thoughout history, including the Field of Palm Trees and the Oasis of Jupiter-Amun.

AT HOME

Chapter 3

What is your house made of? Many people live in wooden homes or apartments, while others live in homes made of brick or cinderblock. Egyptians did not have as many choices. Most of their houses were made out of mud bricks. It may seem that mud bricks would not make a very strong house, but they did.

If Egypt had an extra supply of anything, it was mud and sunshine—the two main things needed to make mud bricks. The mud for the bricks was not just simple dirt and water, though. It was a combination of clay, sand, and chopped straw. Now and then, animal dung and pebbles were included to help make the bricks stronger.

After all the ingredients were stirred together, people kneaded the mud mixture with their feet until it was blended into just the right consistency. Next, the mud was pressed into molds to shape it. The bricks were placed outside in the sunshine to dry and harden. Finally, they were piled on top of each other to make the walls of homes and other buildings.

Would a mud brick home be very large? It could be. The average-sized home for Egyptian families was 13 feet by 66 feet. Inside that 858-square-foot house were two to four rooms—usually a kitchen, a

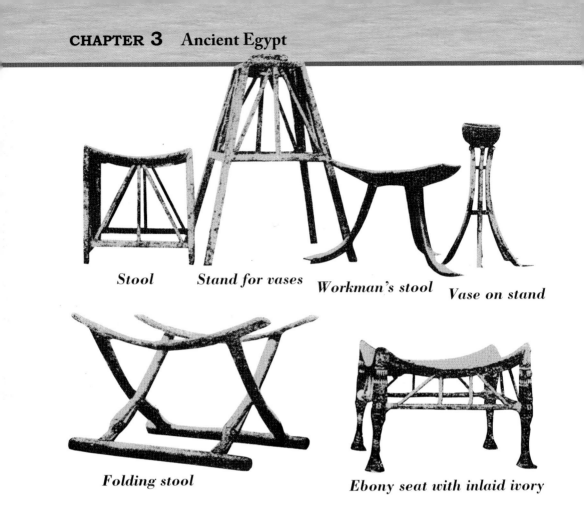

Stool   *Stand for vases* *Workman's stool* *Vase on stand*

Folding stool   *Ebony seat with inlaid ivory*

bedroom, a living room for worshiping gods and ancestors, and a front room for meeting and talking to visitors. A few of the wealthier families had limestone bathrooms, but most families threw their sewage outside in pits or canals. Many homes were two or three stories tall. The bottom floor often contained a cellar for food storage.

The rooms typically held very little furniture, and each piece was quite simple. Beds were usually on short frames, and there were no mattresses. Instead, people slept on flat reed mats. Simple wooden chests held linens and clothing, and handmade baskets held food. Rugs and hangings were put on the walls to give the house color and style. The kitchen often had a clay oven and large pottery jars for holding wine, oil, and grain.

Outside the home, families frequently kept a courtyard with a garden. Flowers were important to the Egyptians. They were used in

funerals and festivals, and as decorations throughout the home. They were also used to make scented oils and perfumes.

Time to Eat!
What is your favorite thing to eat and drink? If you lived in ancient Egypt, your answer would most likely be bread and beer! Everyone drank beer—young and old alike. The ancient Egyptians were actually the ones who invented the drink. They found that soaking grain in water and letting it ferment created this unusual and tasty new beverage. Scientists believe they sometimes heated the mixture and added yeast as it fermented. Egyptian beer was nowhere near as strong as modern beer.

Model of a beer brewery

Bread was served with every meal. A favorite way to eat it was to cut a slice and then cover it with garlic and raw onions. Hopefully, it tasted much better than it smelled!

With all the grain crops grown in Egypt, along with fruit trees, vegetable gardens, and occasionally meat from land, air, and sea, the people had a varied and interesting diet. Without any refrigerators or freezers, food had to be preserved with salt and spices. It was often left out in the sun to dry and become a type of jerky. Records show that Egyptians learned how to be beekeepers, storing their hives in

Egyptian bread, found preserved from sometime between 1070 and 715 BCE

large pottery jars. This provided precious honey for sweetening special dishes.

Women were skilled at finding different ways to cook the food. They figured out how to bake, boil, stew, fry, grill, and roast food in clay ovens or over an open fire.

When it was time to eat, the family would gather together. There was not any silverware, so they used their fingers instead. Before a meal began, everyone dipped their hands in bowls of water to make sure they were clean. Tables were low to the ground, and people did not sit on chairs. They sat cross-legged on the floor on top of reed mats.

Mealtime was family life. Every-many gods for for the people they with.

an important part of one gave thanks to their food—and loved to share it

Egyptian family, sculpture

Up on the Roof

The weather in Egypt was often quite hot. After all, the area was in a desert. During the summer, temperatures would easily reach 100 degrees or more. The sun's burning rays baked everything below it. How could people stay cool when there were no air conditioners or even electric fans? They used their roofs.

To help cope with the heat, most Egyptian homes had flat roofs. Like the walls of the house, the roof was painted with whitewash. This was a white coating made from chalk and lime. The white helped to deflect the sun's heat and keep the house cool.

The roof had many other uses as well. Inside the house, a staircase led up to it. Families would gather on the roof to eat a meal, tell stories, and play games. They often had a small kitchen on the roof for cooking. This way they did not add more heat to their homes when they made a meal.

Egyptian mothers, fathers, children, and relatives would often sit high up on the roof and watch the sun go down. On the hottest nights, they would even take their reed mats and sleep up there under the stars in order to catch the smallest breeze.

Model of an Egyptian home

The Egyptian sky god Horus is shown as a bird of prey. At his feet is King Nectanebo II, under the god's protection. This statue is on display at the Metropolitan Museum of Art in New York.

FOR THE GODS

Chapter 4

In modern times, people follow many different religions. Some go to a church, mosque, or temple as part of their beliefs. Others say special prayers or find other ways to worship. The people of ancient Egypt were very religious people, but their beliefs were a mix of myths and many different gods and goddesses. At one point, they believed in almost one thousand gods.

In modern schools, students learn about many of the reasons things happen in the world. Science explains why the sun rises and sets, why it rains, why the moon seems to change shape, and countless other mysteries that ancient Egyptians did not understand. Instead, they believed that each event was guided, in one way or another, by a specific god or goddess. If they wanted that event to continue, they had to make offerings and say prayers regularly.

Many of the Egyptian deities looked like humans; others looked like animals. Some looked like a combination of both, such as the Sphinx, which has the body of a lion and the face of a person.

Everything that happened in the lives of the Egyptians was explained by the actions of one god or another. Events from terrible disasters

Important Gods and Goddesses in Ancient Egypt

Amun-Re was the supreme sun god and the one deity that most ancient Egyptians felt watched over them. He was usually depicted as a bearded man wearing a hat with two feathers, although sometimes he was pictured as part man, part ram.

Thoth was the god of learning and wisdom and the inventor of writing. Scribes worshiped him. He had a human body but the head of an ibis (a bird).

Anubis was the guardian of tombs and was usually shown as a human with a jackal's head. He was always a part of the mummification process, and Egyptians believed he helped lead the dead on the treacherous path through the underworld.

Hathor was the goddess of love, childbirth, music, and dance. She looked human but had cow horns.

Hapi, the god of the Nile, was a fat, bearded man wearing a crown of flowers. He was said to live in the caves by the river and was responsible for making sure the Nile flooded each year.

Horus, one of the most important gods, was depicted as a man with the head of a creature, usually a falcon or lion. He advised the pharaoh and was known to whisper guidance to him.

Isis, one of the oldest gods, was thought to be a great protector and mother to all other goddesses. She was the female equal of Osiris and was usually pictured as a beautiful woman wearing magnificent, flowing dresses.

Osiris, along with Amun-Re, was an extremely important god. Like Anubis, he was part of the underworld and considered the leader of the gods. He was also the god of farming.

Neith, the goddess of war and weaving, was usually seen as a woman carrying a bow, arrow, and shield.

Isis

Osiris, one of the most powerful gods, was worshiped throughout Egypt. As the son of the earth god Geb, the husband of Isis, and the father of Horus, he served as lord of the dead.

and deaths to abundant crops and healthy babies were due to the deities' decisions. This gave order to the world and reasons to honor and obey the pharaoh.

Inside the Temple

Egyptian temples were not like today's churches. People did not gather there to be closer to their gods, hear a sermon, or pray. In fact, since temples were thought of as the sacred homes of gods and goddesses, only pharaohs and priests were allowed beyond the sanctuary. Commoners did all of their praying at home and generally left the temples alone.

Egyptian gods needed constant attention. They were quite demanding! Before priests could go in to take care of the gods, they had to be purified. Some did this by bathing, while others plunged into water declared to be sacred. Then they gave the gods regular offerings of food and drink.

The priests of this culture had very little contact with people. Instead, they spent their time preparing offerings to the gods, praying, and making sure that the pharaohs and nobles spoke all of the spells

The Temple of Dendur once stood on the Nile River but now is at New York's Metropolitan Museum of Art. Each of the temple's 642 blocks, some weighing more than six tons, were packed into crates and shipped to the United States by the SS Concordia Star.

correctly. It was not unusual for these priests to shave every single bit of body hair, from head to toe. They even cut off their eyelashes! They felt this made them cleaner.

Temples were surrounded by outer walls. A central gate opened onto a courtyard. Beyond this, the temple was very dark. A room called the hypostyle hall was full of columns. It had tiny windows near the ceiling. After that came the sanctuary. It was home to a statue of a god, which was covered in jewels. The Egyptians believed that inside this statue was the god's spirit.

Priests came to the temple in the morning to sing to the god. They bathed it and covered it in fine linens. As incense burned and singers and dancers created music, the priests made offerings of meat, vegetables, and drinks. This ritual was performed three times each day.

At the end of the day, the priests locked the sanctuary doors once more. As they left, they used a broom to sweep away their footsteps just in case a demon came by during the night and spotted them.

The Job of Tears

Men and women were thought of as equal in ancient Egypt. Some women worked outside their homes or owned businesses. They might work as dancers or singers. Some were acrobats! Others were maids, cleaning other people's homes, or nannies, taking care of other people's children. Mothers who were nursing their own babies were often hired to nurse the babies of the nobles. They were called wet nurses. While some women worked as midwives, helping pregnant women deliver their babies, a few went on to become Egyptian doctors.

It was not unusual for women to have businesses that they ran out of their homes. A few made and sold pieces of linen. Others made perfumed oils.

Ancient Egyptian women had many opportunities to thrive outside the household. They were not confined to just childbearing and tending the home.

One of the most unusual jobs a woman could have was a professional mourner. These women were hired by the nobles to go to funerals and cry with great emotion and passion. Just a few tears were not enough, however! Walking behind the coffin, they were expected to tear their clothes, throw themselves on the ground, throw dust over their heads, wail and moan, scratch their skin, and generally make sure everyone knew how tragic it was that this person had died. Their performance was a sign of honor and respect for the deceased and his or her family.

The nobles themselves did not show this much strong emotion because it was considered bad manners. By using professional mourners, they could make a statement about how sad they were without having to shed a single tear.

The women who had this job were sometimes called Hawks of Nephthys. Nephthys was an Egyptian goddess who symbolized sorrow and mourning.

The solid gold coffin of the boy-king Tutankhamun is one of Egypt's most fabulous and famous artifacts. The false beard was added as a sign of power. It was curved to indicate that the young pharaoh had become a god in the afterlife.

LIFE WITH THE PHARAOH

Chapter 5

The pharaoh was worshiped by all the people. To their minds, he was divine and held absolute power. In fact, no one even called him by his name, instead referring to the "palace" or simply the "pharaoh" or "His Majesty" out of respect. He was almost as holy as a god and his every wish was to be obeyed. He was the people's protector, and the only way order was kept was by doing whatever he requested. The priests carried out the pharaoh's wishes. They gave advice, collected taxes, and welcomed visitors to the temple. In addition, they were in charge of the military, and they supervised building projects, organizing huge groups of workers to construct new temples and other buildings.

People who were related to the pharaoh either through blood or marriage usually led an easier life than most. These nobles did not have to work very hard. They had fancy clothes and beautiful jewelry, and went to many parties.

The wealthy nobles typically lived in fancy homes. The houses were made of sun-baked bricks like others, but they also used stone and tile. Unlike the simple homes of the commoners, many of these houses had balconies, religious shrines, long wide hallways, stables, swimming pools, and huge gardens. In fact, it was not unusual for these homes to have 30 rooms or more. The owners hired a variety of painters, sculptors, weavers, and other craftsmen to decorate their luxurious houses. Of course, they also brought in a number of servants to cook and clean for them.

One thing nobles loved to do was celebrate! They hosted dances, parties, and feasts. They dressed in their best clothes, ate gourmet food, and watched entertainers. At a pharaoh's party, guests were often welcomed with garlands of flowers and scented water. They ate exotic meals like antelope, gazelle, or ibex, as well as yeast bread. Everything was chased down with barley ale (similar to beer) or wine made from grapes, figs, dates, or pomegranates. As everyone ate, they were entertained by energetic acrobats and musicians playing flutes, drums, and harps.

An ibex

What happened when a pharaoh died? It was an event! To honor his wisdom, power and importance, he was often housed in one of the most magnificent tombs ever created: the pyramid. These unique memorials not only held the body of the pharaoh, encased in jewel-encrusted, gold-covered coffins called sarcophagi, but they also held many of his greatest treasures for use in the afterlife. While one room was known as the burial chamber, others were created for separate purposes. For example, an "offering chapel" was created for food donations; these would keep the pharaoh fed on his way to the other side.

Pyramids are such distinct buildings that it is hard to imagine ancient Egypt without picturing them. As one of the most unusual constructions in world history, they have confused experts for centuries as to how they were built. How could such massive buildings be created in a time without power tools and earth moving equipment?

Some unusual theories have been handed down through the years as possible explanations. One recurring theme has been that the pyramids were built by an alien race from another planet! Only creatures of more advanced knowledge and skills could have built something so huge and

The Great Sphinx and one of the pyramids at Giza were built during Khafre's rule. The pyramid is immense—standing 450 feet tall and almost 700 feet wide at the base, or about the size of two football fields placed end to end. Khafre's father, Khufu, built the even larger Great Pyramid.

The Great Pyramid of Khufu, in Giza, is the only Wonder of the Ancient World that has survived, but other pyramids were of great importance as well. The pyramid of Djoser at Sakkara was the first one ever built in Egypt, and those in Dahshur show how the builders tried different styles, methods, and materials until they figured out the best combination for creating the most durable buildings. The Pyramid of Ahmose at Abydos was the last pyramid ever built by royal command. The Valley of the Kings in Thebes (Luxor) holds many tombs, including Tutankhamun's. The Great Sphinx (below) symbolizes the power of the pharaohs. Its eyes are over 6 feet (2 meters) high.

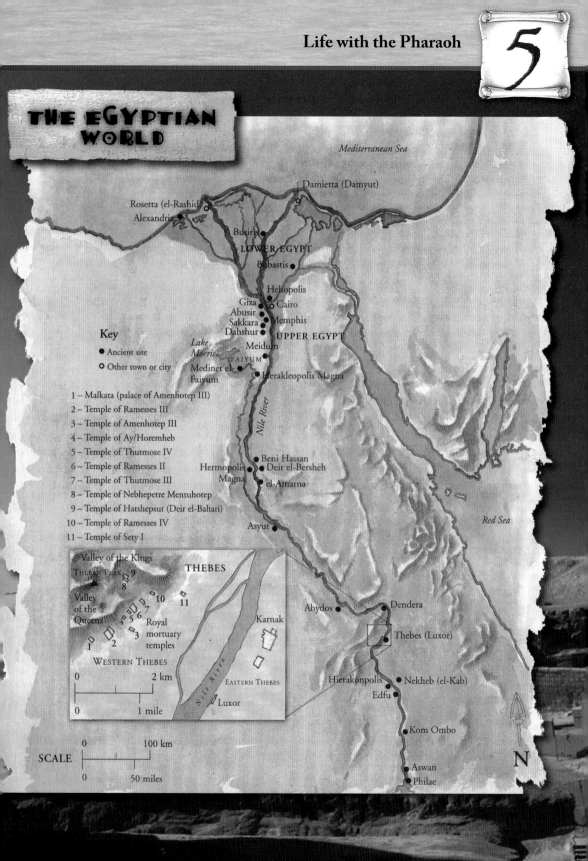

THE EGYPTIAN WORLD

Mediterranean Sea

Damietta (Damyut)

Rosetta (el-Rashid)
Alexandria

Busiris

LOWER EGYPT

Bubastis

Heliopolis

Giza
Abusir
Sakkara
Dahshur

Cairo
Memphis

UPPER EGYPT

Meidum

Lake Moeris
FAIYUM

Medinet el-Faiyum

Herakleopolis Magna

Key

● Ancient site

○ Other town or city

1 – Malkata (palace of Amenhotep III)
2 – Temple of Ramesses III
3 – Temple of Amenhotep III
4 – Temple of Ay/Horemheb
5 – Temple of Thutmose IV
6 – Temple of Ramesses II
7 – Temple of Thutmose III
8 – Temple of Nebhepetre Mentuhotep
9 – Temple of Hatshepsut (Deir el-Bahari)
10 – Temple of Ramesses IV
11 – Temple of Sety I

Nile River

Beni Hassan
Hermopolis Magna
Deir el-Bersheh
el-Amarna

Asyut

Valley of the Kings
THEBAN PEAK 9
8 **THEBES**
Valley of the Queens
10
6 5
7
11

Karnak

4 5 3 Royal mortuary temples
1 2

WESTERN THEBES

0 _____ 2 km

0 _____ 1 mile

Nile River

EASTERN THEBES

Luxor

Abydos

Dendera

Thebes (Luxor)

Red Sea

Hierakonpolis
Edfu

Nekheb (el-Kab)

Kom Ombo

SCALE

0 _____ 100 km

0 _____ 50 miles

Aswan
Philae

N

The entrance to one of the tombs at Giza. The three pyramids there—of pharaohs Khufu, Khafre, and Menkaure—were built more than 4500 years ago.

complicated, theorists claim. What evidence do they have to back up their claims? People are still waiting for them to find it.

It has taken years of research—and not a small amount of debate—but historians are now fairly certain that the Great Pyramid in Giza was built by approximately 25,000 workers (not slaves) over a period of 20 years or more. The workers were divided up by the kind of work they did. The majority of them built ramps, made stone and copper tools, mixed mortar, and provided supplies to others, such as food and clothing. Another 4,000 worked in the quarries, smashing stones, while others hauled it on wooden sleds to the right site. About 5,000 of the workers were considered permanent. They and their families lived in villages surrounding the pyramids. The rest of the workers were temporary, working for a few months and then being replaced by others. They were typically paid through rations, such as loaves of bread and tankards of beer. Once Egyptians finished their work on the pyramids, they usually returned to their homes loaded with food and drink, as well as many new skills.

FYInfo

Egyptian Slaves

What was it like to be a slave in ancient Egypt? Experts have asked that question for many years. Through the ages, they have come up with new ideas. They believe that, in many ways, Egyptian slavery was different from the type that was practiced in the early United States. Unlike in other cultures, everyone in Egypt had some level of civil rights.

Although many movies have been made showing mistreated slaves being forced to push huge stone blocks up ramps to build the pyramids, this is Hollywood's image, not history's truth. There is nothing in any of the archaeological or historical records to support that this ever happened.

Without a doubt, there were people in Egypt who were owned by the wealthy and who could be sold to another party. Owners were allowed to rent these workers out to someone else, as well as to give the people their freedom if they so chose. On the other hand, these workers could also own homes and land, marry whom they wanted, and, if they earned enough, hire their own slaves.

The majority of the people working as slaves were foreign prisoners who had been captured in battle. Others were people trying to work off debts or even convicted criminals who were sentenced to work for others. These slaves worked in the households of the nobles, as well as in the fields, mines, quarries, and temples. They cleaned homes, dug irrigation ditches, and built temples. They harvested crops and helped priests carry out their rituals.

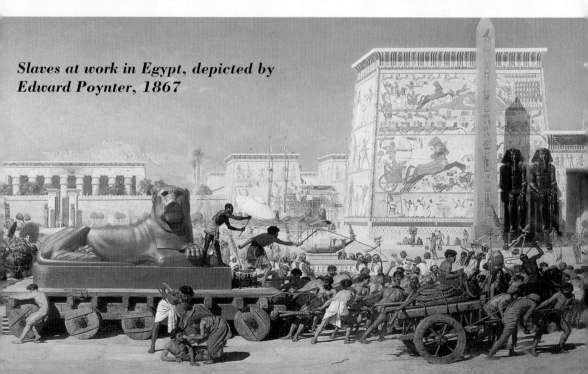

Slaves at work in Egypt, depicted by Edward Poynter, 1867

A diorama in the Royal Ontario Museum displays an Egyptian noblewoman using a mirror to apply her makeup, much like women do today. Colorful jewelry, stark white linens, and face paint were marks of high status.

LOOKiNG GooD

Chapter 6

Looking attractive was extremely important to the Egyptians, whether they were workers or royalty. Their appearance often reflected their status or how others saw them. Because of this, men and women put ribbons and decorations in their hair or wigs; applied brightly colored makeup to their eyes, cheeks and lips; and added jewelry to their necks, wrists, and ankles.

It was not easy to keep looking and smelling good in the overwhelming desert heat of Egypt. People could not hop in the shower whenever they got sweaty. There was not any deodorant to grab and apply. Some women got around that by putting cones of scented animal fat on top of their wigs. As the day got hotter, the fat would melt and release perfume. Many people would bathe in the river, and most homes had a jug of water for washing at home. They did not have any soap, so instead they used a cleansing cream made from oil, lime, and perfume. A number of people carried small glass containers with perfume in them so that they could add a few dabs here and there when they most needed it.

The heat and the strong winds were hard on people's skin. To help keep it soft, they would rub their skin with oils and lotions made from a combination of animal fat and crushed flowers. Lotions were considered so important that some people's wages were paid in these special creams.

Wearing the right clothes was a big part of keeping cool. While children tended to be nude until they became teenagers, adults usually wore linen clothes, which were made from the fibers of flax plants that grew in the area. Flax grew about two feet tall, with blue flowers and small

Flax

The length of men and women's skirts changed with time. During the time of the Old Kingdom (c.2575–2150 BCE), skirts were short, while in the Middle Kingdom (c.1975–1640 BCE), they went to the calf.

leaves. Turning this plant into a piece of clothing was a complex process. First, it had to be pulled, dried, shredded, and soaked. The fibers were separated and then attached to a spindle, which was used to twist the fibers into a strong thread. Then the thread was loaded onto a loom for weaving.

Both men and women wore long, flowing dresses, but men also sometimes wore loincloths or short kilt-like skirts and no shirts. Almost all of the clothing was white—once again to help deflect the sun's hot rays. As the sun went down and the temperatures began to cool, some people would throw a cloak around their shoulders to ward off the evening chill. Since the ancient Egyptians didn't have washing machines to keep their white clothes clean,

Beadnet dress, made of faience, and dating back to the 4th dynasty

Broad collar and ankle bracelet, 5th dynasty, made of faience

Golden funeral sandals from 1479-1425 BCE, at the Metropolitan Museum of Art, New York City

they had to wash the clothes often in the river, pound them on a stone, and then bleach them in the sun.

Most of the time, Egyptians walked around barefoot. When they did put on shoes—to protect their feet from the hot desert sand, or to keep safe from the bites of snakes and scorpions—they wore sandals made from reeds. The nobles wore them also, but theirs were typically made of leather. These sandals looked a great deal like today's flip-flops. Gold sandals were placed on the feet of the dead.

To check their look, Egyptians used large pieces of highly polished metal as mirrors. This way they could ensure they put on their makeup and clothes just the way they planned.

Egyptian Makeup

If you look at drawings of Egyptian figures, one of the first things you might notice is their eyes. They seem to leap off the page because they are colorful and often circled in black.

Both men and women in ancient Egypt wore eye makeup on a daily basis. They did it to look nice—but it was much more than that. They wore it for health reasons. They wore it for

A woman carefully gets ready for her day.

magical reasons. They wore it for protection! The eye makeup had elements in it that helped protect the eyes from intense sunlight. Lining the eyes in black supposedly kept the person safe from evil spirits and demons as well. It was so important to the Egyptians that traces of it have been found in many graves and tombs in containers next to the body.

The eye makeup available in ancient Egypt was not like today's, of course. It only came in a few colors and had to be made from either copper or lead. It did not come in easy packages, either. Instead, the minerals had to be mined, ground into a powder, and then mixed with animal fat in order to get it to stick to the eyelids. Everyone, from the slaves to the nobles, wore makeup. The only difference was that the nobles kept theirs in beautiful carved boxes, and the commoners in rough wooden bowls.

While eye makeup was worn every day, on special occasions, the Egyptians also wore blush on their lips and cheeks. It came from red iron clay found in the area. A dye called henna was used on their nails and hair to change the color.

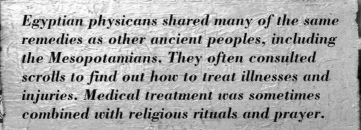

Egyptian physicans shared many of the same remedies as other ancient peoples, including the Mesopotamians. They often consulted scrolls to find out how to treat illnesses and injuries. Medical treatment was sometimes combined with religious rituals and prayer.

BEYOND DEATH

Chapter 7

Were Egyptians healthy? In many ways, they were. They ate a rich and varied diet. They certainly got enough physical exercise and sunshine every day. Of course, there were times when someone got sick or injured. When that happened, the person could go to a doctor. Ancient Egyptian doctors knew how to heal wounds, mend broken bones, and treat basic diseases.

Doctors were a fascinating mixture of trained scientists and magicians. It was not unusual for doctors to also be priests. As they examined a patient, put on a splint, rubbed on an ointment, or prepared an herb mixture for someone, they often also sent up a few spells to whatever god or goddess seemed best. They frequently blamed an evil spirit or furious deity for causing the health problem in the first place.

When doctors saw a patient, first they would determine if the person's condition was curable, incurable, or uncertain. They would check a person's pulse and even his or her reflexes. What did doctors give their patients before the days of aspirin and bandages? Egyptian doctors made medicine from more than 600 different ingredients. Some of these ingredients sound worse than the condition they were being used to treat. For example, a potion might include myrrh, malachite, garlic, figs, dates, honey, dill, or cucumbers. It might also have dung, blood, and animal fat. The cure for indigestion, for example, was to take a crushed hog's tooth, place it inside sugar cakes, and eat the cakes for four days in a row. Burns were treated with the breast milk from a baby boy's mother, combined with gum resin and the hair of a ram—plus a sincere prayer sent to Horus to please extinguish the terrible fire. The tools Egyptian doctors used ranged from scalpels and knives to tweezers and thorns. With these things, they were able to perform simple surgeries.

There were different levels of doctors, according to how much training they had. The *senenu* were the least educated. They were little more than scribes who had read a few medical papers. The *sau* were magical doctors who specialized in treating anyone who seemed to be ill as a punishment from one of the gods. They were trained in the House of Life, a temple school for doctors and priests. Higher-level doctors were called masters, and of course, the pharaoh had his own personal physician to take care of him and his family.

The Edwin Smith papyrus, the oldest surviving surgical document from around 1600 BCE, describes the treatment of 48 medical problems in great detail, such as closing wounds with sutures, and curing infections with honey and moldy bread.

Egyptian physicians could even replace missing body parts now and then. This prosthetic toe, carved from wood and attached to the foot with a leather wrapping, is on display at the Egyptian Museum in Cairo.

Sometimes doctors looked to a patient's dreams to figure out what was wrong with him. They would look for a theme or a message from one of the gods. If a person dreamed about a dwarf, for example, it meant half of his life was already over and bad times were ahead.

Can you guess what the biggest health problem was for the Egyptians? It was their teeth! They did not have cavities because there was very little sugar in their diets. All they had was a little honey now and then. The problem came from the bread they ate. The flour they used was made by grinding the wheat by hand with a stone. In the process of grinding it, sand would get into the flour—sometimes quite a bit of it. The sand would be baked into the bread and as people ate it, it would slowly grind down at the enamel on their teeth. By the time they were adults, the enamel was worn away and the teeth would get infected. The Egyptians lost a lot of teeth that way!

Ancient Egypt's version of a makeup tray was found in this toilet box. It holds alabaster jars, glass bottles, and faience vessels designed for holding ointments for use in the afterlife.

Life beyond Death

Egyptians loved their lives—but they looked forward to the afterlife almost as much. To them, death was simply a ticket to another life in another world. They lost their souls, or *ka,* for only a short time. It would be returned to them once they were on the other side.

The people spent a great deal of effort and time making sure that when they appeared in the afterlife, they were completely prepared with everything they would need. When they were buried, their relatives made sure to include extra clothes, food, and other valuables in the tomb with them. The more valuables a family had, the more they could prepare their loved ones for life after death.

When a rich person died, his body was taken to the Nile's west bank to be turned into a mummy. When the process was finished, the body was put into a coffin, along with all the belongings it would need for the trip into the afterlife. Once the tomb was sealed, it was time to make the journey to the other side.

It was not an easy trip. The deceased person had to pass through many gates, and each one was protected by a ferocious and threatening monster. Once the person reached the place of judgment, he had to list a number of sins in front of 42 judges and then swear he had not committed any of them. Anubis would take the person's heart and place it on holy scales to see if the person was telling the truth. If the person had truly lived a good life, the heart would be very light and he could pass on to meet his ancestors in the next world. However, if the heart was heavy, it would be gobbled up by Ammut, a crocodile-headed monster. It was not the end that any Egyptian wanted to face.

Making Mummies

The Egyptians are known for many things, but perhaps one of the most famous is how they treated their most important dead so that the deceased would not decay in their tombs. Making a mummy was not an easy or fast process. In fact, from beginning to end, it took 70 days. It was also not a procedure for the fainthearted!

To start the process, the embalmers, or the people who took care of dead bodies, would place the body on a slanted table so that all of the blood could drain out. Next, they would remove the brain. They did this by shoving a long, sharp hook up through the nose and pulling it back out again. The Egyptians believed that the brain did not do anything important, so they did not worry about taking care of it. Instead, they thought the heart was the center of all intelligence and emotions.

Once the brain was removed, the embalmers cut open the body in order to remove other internal organs. These were placed inside canopic jars. The heart was left inside, however, because it was needed during the journey to the afterlife. Its weight determined how sinful a person had been in life and whether he or she was destined for eternity—or much worse.

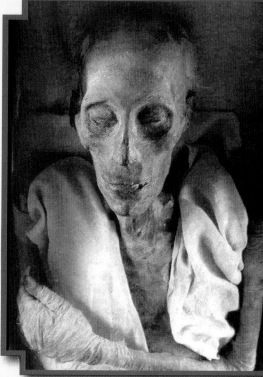

Mummy of
Pharaoh Ramesses II

Once the organs had been removed, the embalmers covered the body with salt inside and out, then left it to dry for between 40 and 70 days. The salt preserved the body, preventing decay. When the drying period was over, melted tree sap was poured over the entire body to seal the skin.

The body was placed in a coffin and surrounded by sand, spices, scented oil, and fine linens. Magic amulets were placed in the coffin for protection. A beautiful funeral mask, often painted and decorated with gems, was placed on the person's face, and then the coffin was closed. Often this coffin would be placed inside another one, or several, depending on the importance of the person being buried. The Egyptians mummified some of their most important people. They didn't stop there, though. They also mummified their cats, birds, dogs, and even bulls.

Make an Egyptian Reed Boat

The Egyptians used small, personal boats for short trips and to run errands. Here is how you can make your own out of a few simple materials.

You will need:
16 drinking straws that bend
Narrow masking tape
White string
Scissors
A large bowl
An adult

Here is what to do:
1. Pull on the short end of one of the straws so that the crinkled, bendy part is pulled out as far as it will go. Repeat until all 16 straws are done.
2. Line the straws up next to each other, with eight pointing one way and eight pointing the opposite way, in alternating order.

3. Tape the straws together with the masking tape. Start in the middle. Add a strip on each end, near the bendy crinkles. Tape them firmly so that there are no gaps between the straws.
4. Cut a piece of string about four inches long.
5. Wrap the string around one end of the straws and tie them together. Repeat at the other end.
6. Fill a large bowl with water. Place the boat in it and watch it float.

TIMELINE

BCE

3100–2950   Late predynastic period; the Egyptian state is established

2950–2575   Early dynastic period (1st–3rd dynasties); the first pyramid is built

2575–2150   Old Kingdom (4th–8th dynasties; the Great Pyramids of Giza are built

2125–1975   1st intermediate period (9th–11th dynasties); Egypt splits into two smaller states.

1975–1640   Middle Kingdom (11th–14th dynasties); Mentuhotep reunites Egypt

1930–1520   2nd intermediate period (15th–17th dynasties)

1539–1075   New Kingdom (18th–20th dynasties); including the rule of Tutankhamun and Ramesses II

1075–715	3rd intermediate period (21st–25th dynasties); Egypt is conquered by the Nubians
715–332	Late Period (20th–30th dynasties); Egypt is captured by Persia, then regains its independence
CE	
332–395	Greco-Roman Period; Egypt occupied by Alexander the Great, Cleopatra VII reigns; Rosetta Stone is carved

Scholars divide antiquity into smaller periods of time, according to which family was in power. Not all scholars divide time the same way. Some eras are referred to as periods, while others are called dynasties based on who was ruling. This book uses both titles as employed by the BBC History scholars.

FURTHER READING

Books

Cobblestone Publishing. *If I Were a Kid in Ancient Egypt*. Chicago: Cricket Books, 2007.

Hart, George. *Ancient Egypt*. New York: DK Children, 2008.

Shearer, Cynthia. *The Greenleaf Guide to Ancient Egypt*. Lebanon, Tennessee: Greenleaf Press, 2007.

Steele, Philip. *Step into Ancient Egypt*. Lanham, Maryland: Southwater, 2008.

Van Vleet, Carmella. *Explore Ancient Egypt: 25 Great Projects, Activities, Experiments*. Nomad, Colorado Nomad Press, 2008.

Works Consulted

Brier, Bob, and Hoyt Hobbs. *Daily Life of the Ancient Egyptians*. Westport, Connecticut: Greenwood Press. 1999.

David, Rosalie. *Handbook of Life in Ancient Egypt*. New York: Facts on File, 2003.

Gahlin, Lucia. *Egypt: Gods, Myths and Religion*. (Anness Publishing Ltd: New York) 2002.

Mertz, Barbara. *Red Land, Black Land*. New York: HarperCollins Books, 2008.

Shaw, Ian. *Exploring Ancient Egypt*. New York: Oxford University Press, 2003.

On the Internet

Ancient Egypt for Kids
    http://egypt.mrdonn.org/
Kidipede's Ancient Egypt
    http://www.historyforkids.org/learn/egypt/
KidsKonnect.com Ancient Egypt
    http://www.kidskonnect.com/content/view/253/27/
King Tut One.com
    http://www.kingtutone.com/kids/
Social Studies for Kids: Ancient Egypt
    http://www.socialstudiesforkids.com/subjects/ancientegypt.htm

GLOSSARY

afterlife (AF-ter-lyf)—What some cultures believe a person experiences after they die.

amulet (AM-yoo-let)—A necklace worn to protect its wearer.

demotic (de-MAH-tik)—An everyday, casual form of the Greek language.

dynasty (DY-nuh-stee)—A sequence of rulers from the same family.

ferment (FER-ment)—To convert sugar to alcohol.

flax—A plant whose fibers are used to make linen, a type of cloth.

hieroglyphs (HY-roh-glifs)—Symbols that represent letters and sounds.

papyrus (puh-PY-rus)—A tall aquatic plant used to make writing paper; also, the paper made with papyrus.

pharaoh (FAH-roh)—An Egyptian king.

sanctuary (SANK-choo-wayr-ee)—A sacred, holy, or safe place.

shadoof (SHAH-doof)—A machine consisting of a pole, bucket, and counterweight that is used to dip water from a well or spring and transfer it to fields.

vizier (vih-ZEER)—An ancient Egyptian priest.

afterlife   36, 38, 54, 55

Ahmose   40, 41

Amenhotep III   17, 41

Ammut   54

Amun   20, 21, 24, 32, 33

Amun-Re   32

Anubis   32, 54

appearance   20, 38, 45, 49

Beautiful Feast of Opet   20

Beautiful Feast of the Valley   22

"black land"   10

Bonaparte, Napoleon   23

cats   18, 19, 55

Champollion, Jean François   23

climate   29

clothing   20, 44, 45–48, 54

commoners   13, 15, 37

corn   8–9

crafts   14–15, 38

crops   9, 10, 11, 27, 43

Djoser, 40, 41

doctors   35, 50, 51–53

Edwin Smith papyrus   52

Egypt, map of   41

faience   47, 54

families   19–20, 22, 28, 29, 42, 54

farming   6–10, 11, 32

festivals   20, 22

flax   46–47

food   15, 27–28, 34, 38, 51, 54

funerals   48, 54

furniture   26, 28

games and play   15–16, 17, 20

Geb   33

Giza   39, 40, 41, 42

Hapi   32

Hathor   32

Hatshepsut   41

hieroglyphs   14, 23

homes   24, 25–26, 29, 37–38

Horemheb   41

Horus   30, 32, 33, 52

House of Life   52

Isis   32, 33

jewelry   14–15, 38, 44, 45, 47

jobs   13–15, 35

Karnak Temple   20, 21

Khafre   39, 42

Khufu   39, 40, 42

lock of youth   20

lotion   46

makeup   14, 44, 45, 48, 49, 54

marriage   22, 43

mummies   18, 32, 54, 55

music   16, 34, 38

Nebhepetre Mentuhotep   41

Nectanebo, King   30

Neith   32

Nephthys   35

INDEX

Nile River 9–10, 11, 16, 20, 32, 41, 48, 54
nilometer 11
nobles 14–15, 35, 37, 43, 49
Osiris 17, 32, 33
papyrus 15, 16
perfume 27, 35, 45
pets 19, 55
pharaohs 13, 20, 32, 33, 36, 37–38, 39, 40–41, 42, 52
pottery 26, 28,
priests 13–14, 33–34, 37, 43
professional mourners 35
pyramids 11, 38, 39, 40, 41, 42, 43
Ramesses II 41, 55
Ramesses III 41
Ramesses IV 41
"red land" 10
religion 20, 21, 22, 28, 30, 31, 32, 33–34, 35, 50, 51, 53, 54
Rosetta Stone 23
school 19
scribes 12, 13–14, 32, 52
Seated Scribe 12
senet 17
Sety I 41
sewage 26
shadoof 10

Shemu 6
Siwa Oasis 24
slaves 6, 42, 43, 49
sphinx 31, 32, 39, 40
Temple of Dendur 34
temples 34, 37, 43
Thoth 32
Thutmose IV 41
Tutankhamun 37, 40
underworld 32, 33
vases 15
viziers (and see priests) 13
wigs 14, 45
women 28, 35
Young, Thomas 23

ABOUT THE AUTHOR

Tamra Orr is the author of almost 200 nonfiction books for readers of all ages, including more than two dozen for Mitchell Lane Publishers. She has written about many different countries and cultures throughout the world. It is one of her favorite ways to travel! Several of her titles have won awards. Orr has a degree in English and Secondary Education from Ball State University in Muncie, Indiana. She lives in the Pacific Northwest with her four kids, husband, dog, and cat. When she isn't researching and writing a book, she is usually reading one or walking outside to gaze at the beautiful snow-covered mountains.